PAPER YACHTS

PAPER YACHTS

STREAMLINED DESIGNS AND WATER-RESISTANT TEMPLATES TO MAKE AND SAIL

NIC COMPTON & NICK ROBINSON

Ivy Press

First published in the UK in 2009 by
Ivy Press
210 High Street, Lewes
East Sussex BN7 2NS, UK
www.ivy-group.co.uk

British Library Cataloguing-in-Publication Data
A catalogue record for this book is available from the British Library

ISBN: 978-1-905695-86-7

Ivy Press
This book was conceived, designed, and produced by Ivy Press

Creative Director *Peter Bridgewater*
Publisher *Jason Hook*
Editorial Director *Tom Kitch*
Art Director *Wayne Blades*
Senior Project Editor *Polita Caaveiro*
Designers *Ginny Zeal and Kate Haynes*
Illustrator *Nick Robinson*
Templates *Adam Elliott*

All origami designs copyright © 2009 by Nick Robinson (www.origami.me.co.uk),
except "Open 60," copyright © 2009 by Maarten Van Gelder.

PICTURE CREDITS

Mark Lloyd/DPPI/OC Events p.32; Mark Lloyd/Oman Sail p.33 (left); Vincent Curutchet/DPPI/OC
Events p.33 (bottom, far bottom), p.35 (bottom); onEdition/OC Events p.34, p.35 (left); Thierry
Seray/DPPI/OC Events p.35 (far left); Carlo Borlenghi/ACM2007 p.12, p.13 (all images); Christian
Février/Bluegreen p.8, p.9 (bottom left, bottom); Erwan Quéméré/Bluegreen p.11 (right); Richard
Langdon/Bluegreen p.11 (bottom); Nic Compton/Salty Dog Media p.10; Vanessa Bird/Salty Dog
Media p.11 (far right); Rick Tomlinson/Volvo Ocean Race p.2, p.27 (bottom right, bottom), p.28,
p.29 (bottom left, top left); Rick Tomlinson p.24, p.25 (bottom left, bottom, left), p.27 (left), p.29
(left); Oskar Kihlborg/Volvo Ocean Race p.6; Dave Kneale/Volvo Ocean Race p.26, p.27 (bottom
left), p.29 (top); John S. Johnston (c1839-1899, Public Domain), p.9 (left); All images on pp.16-21
are courtesy of onEdition.

Printed in China

10 9 8 7 6 5 4 3 2 1

Contents

TOP ABN AMRO 2 *heads for the Southern Ocean from Wellington, New Zealand after the start of the fourth leg of the Volvo Open 70 race in 2005-06.*

These are exciting times for yacht racing. The America's Cup class boat is about to adopt a new, bigger, and more exciting design; an unprecedented number of Open 60s have been built for the next Vendée Globe round-the-world race; and the latest generation of Volvo Ocean Race competitors now have a new route through parts of Asia. Meanwhile, a new class of catamarans, the Extreme 40s, has been launched with high-profile sponsors and a vibrant, international race circuit.

Of course, not everyone can afford to take part in sailing at the highest level, but why should anyone miss out on the adrenalin-fueled excitement and tactical challenges of racing yachts? That is why we have recreated the excitement of big boat racing in a small boat format. But these are not just any paper boats. These are stripped-down versions of the most competitive yachts on the planet, raced by the top sailors on major ocean voyages or short-tacking around the cans. These paper yachts are designed to be sailed hard and to be raced hard, so there's no room for complacency!

THE FOUR CLASSES

We have chosen four classes of boats, each with its own construction techniques and special sailing characteristics. Most sailors will be familiar with the America's Cup Class (ACC), the Open 60s, the Volvo Open 70s, and the Extreme 40s, but how many can say they've sailed them—let alone owned a fleet of them? You'll find that the skills needed in your miniature boatyard are closely related to the skills you'll need on your real boat. Ensuring your origami folds are sharp enough to create a beautifully streamlined sail will equip you with the dexterity required to put a stitch in the full-size version next time it is needed. With four boats in each class, there are enough teams for some serious match racing or, thanks to our simple handicapping rules, for a mixed-class regatta.

RULES OF RACING

In time, the committed paper yachtsman or yachtswoman will learn to get the most out of their dainty craft, by adjusting the ballast to suit the weather conditions and honing their sailing tactics. Unlike most racing circuits, we believe that rules are there to be broken and we actively encourage sailors to use wile and cunning to beat their fellow competitors. The only laws that are sacrosanct are the rules of the sea (see International Convention for the Safety of Life at Sea [SOLAS], 1974, www.imo.org). Also, the jury's decision is final.

Perhaps the best part of owning your own fleet of paper yachts is being able to experience the same adrenalin rush as those Southern Ocean sailors, as your miniature Open 60 surfs down a wave. (It is estimated that the effect of a 6" [15cm] wave on one of these paper crafts is the equivalent of a 60' [18m] ocean roller on their full-size counterparts.) Feel the euphoria as your miniature America's Cup yacht cuts across the bow of a rival on starboard tack and wins the ACC race series. Imagine all this without having to endure months of sleep deprivation or having to do the fundraising necessary to put together a multi-million-dollar race campaign.

RULES OF ORIGAMI

The word origami means "folding paper" and defines the limits of the art. In other words, paper models are made by folding techniques alone, not by using glue or scissors. This restriction forces the designer to engineer creative solutions to problems, rather than assembling the piece in kit form. In fact, the very restriction of the art is the appeal for many folders; overcoming a complex paper-folding challenge brings great satisfaction.

This is also true for designing origami boats that float. Aside from the folding material needing to be water-resistant, there are two essential problems: buoyancy and the center of gravity. The first can be addressed by opening and rounding the hulls where possible, which makes the boat float better. The second is somewhat harder. When dealing with a material as light as paper, it's easy for the structure to become unbalanced; simply an extra layer or two of paper at one end of the boat will make it float lower at that end. Short of adding undesirable levels of complexity to the folding sequence, the best solution is to add ballast in the form of small coins, paper clips, and so on. Inevitably, these paper yachts will be strongly affected by the wind and can easily capsize. Again, the simplest solution is to add ballast to counteract the effect of the wind—just as a real yacht would.

Origami instructions use a set of diagramming symbols (see right). Once you have mastered them, you can create four miniatures of real racing yachts in each class using the templates at the back of this book. However, it is best that you practice folding with scrap paper first!

DIAGRAMMING SYMBOLS

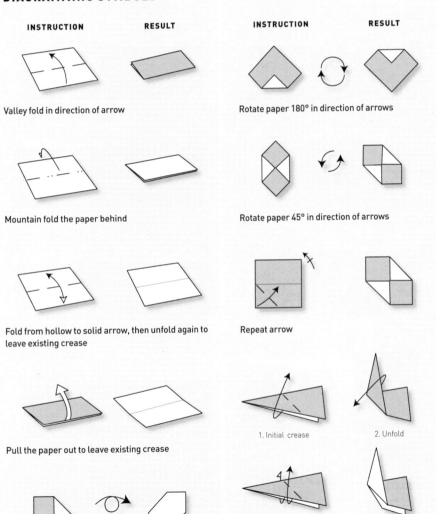

INSTRUCTION   **RESULT**

Valley fold in direction of arrow

Mountain fold the paper behind

Fold from hollow to solid arrow, then unfold again to leave existing crease

Pull the paper out to leave existing crease

Turn the paper over front to back

INSTRUCTION   **RESULT**

Rotate paper 180° in direction of arrows

Rotate paper 45° in direction of arrows

Repeat arrow

1. Initial crease
2. Unfold
3. Open and wrap around outside
4. Complete

Outside reverse

America's Cup

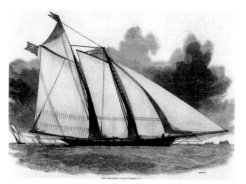

TOP *The schooner America beat all comers in a race around the Isle of Wight in 1851. The event is named after this yacht and not the country.*

The America's Cup is the longest continually running sporting event in the world. It is the most prized trophy in the sailing world and the contest that most professional sailors aspire to compete in at some point in their careers. While often described as elitist, the America's Cup has inspired many otherwise sensible people to spend fortunes in their quest to participate. It has destroyed as many sailing careers as it has made, and is as famous for its drama in the courtroom as on the water. Meet the America's Cup.

When the Swiss team of *Alinghi* won the America's Cup in March 2003, the first thought on everyone's mind was: Where will the next Cup be held? According to the rules that govern how the Cup is organized, the yacht club of the winning team is responsible for hosting the following event. Yet, while *Alinghi* and the Société Nautique de Genève (SNG) had mounted a formidable challenge and won the Cup by 5–0, the yacht club, based in land-locked Switzerland, could hardly claim to have "an ocean water course on the sea," as specified in the rules. The solution was to move its operation to the Mediterranean port of Valencia, in Spain. It was the first time in the Cup's 156-year history that the event would be held in Europe.

The 2007 challenge was widely reckoned to be the best America's Cup ever. A new harbor was built to host the event in Valencia's former commercial port, and an estimated 1.8 million visitors came, generating an income of some $4 billion for the region. Better still, the racing was closely contested and, despite sometimes lucky weather conditions, produced some genuinely exciting competition. Eleven teams took part in the Louis Vuitton challenger series to determine who would take on *Alinghi* in the America's Cup proper. After three months of sailing, Emirates Team New Zealand beat off all its rivals to race in the Cup, only to be beaten by *Alinghi* by 5–2. The Cup was staying in Europe.

A LEGAL CHALLENGE

It should have been a straightforward repeat performance for the 2009 Cup, with the SNG once again hosting the event in Valencia. And, barely had the sails been lowered, than *Alinghi* had signed a deal with Spanish challengers *Desafio Español* to do just that. The trouble was, the Spanish team's yacht club had only been formed a few weeks before. When *Alinghi* published a racing Protocol that many described as "one-sided" and favoring the defender (i.e. *Alinghi*), the American BMW Oracle team issued a writ in the New York Supreme Court to prevent the contest going ahead. The legal proceedings put the Cup in a state of limbo for over a year, and made it unlikely any event would take place in 2009.

But it was not the first time the world's most prestigious sailing event has been held up by legal wrangles. The America's Cup started in August 1851 when the schooner *America* crossed the Atlantic and moored up off Cowes on the Isle of Wight, the yachting capital of the UK. It was also the year of the Great Exhibition, and a group of American entrepreneurs wanted to show what their country had to offer in the way of boatbuilding skills.

LEFT *The* Volunteer, *a 108' (33m) yacht, easily won the seventh America's Cup in 1887.*

BOTTOM LEFT *The J-class* Velsheda *crosses* Shamrock V *with right of way.* Velsheda *is rigged with three headsails— a feature on the J-class yachts until 1934.*

BOTTOM *The* Rainbow, *one of the legendary J-Class yachts that raced the America's Cup in the 1930s. In 1934, she beat the British* Endeavour *yacht by 4–2.*

The Oldest Sporting Trophy

What they got was an invitation to take part in a race around the Isle of Wight, the prize being a rather fussy silver cup some 2' 3" (68cm) tall and weighing 8lb 6oz (3.8kg).

America beat the other fourteen yachts entered in the race for the so-called "100 Guinea Cup" by a wide margin, and took the Cup home to New York. There, a set of rules, called the Deed of Gift, was devised to govern the race in the future.

THE CUP GOES LEGAL

The Cup's reputation for "going legal" started with its second challenge in 1871, when British railway entrepreneur James Ashbury returned for another attempt, having been soundly beaten the year before by a whole fleet of yachts from the New York Yacht Club. After consulting his lawyers, he insisted on a one-to-one duel for his second challenge, and then disputed the score and argued with the racing committee. He was beaten 4–1, and limped home protesting at America's "unsportsmanlike" behavior.

The Cup then saw a series of failed challenges, mainly from Britain, in increasingly large yachts, culminating in the entry of the 202' (61.5m) *Reliance* of 1903, the largest boat to ever compete in the event. One of its most persistent suitors was the "king's grocer," Sir Thomas Lipton, who mounted five challenges between 1899 and 1930—only to be beaten at every attempt.

THE GOLDEN ERA

TOP Velsheda *is the only J-Class yacht not to be built as an America's Cup contender. Now restored and converted into a modern super-yacht, she's pictured sailing off Antigua.*

Lipton's final challenge was raced on the new J-Class yachts, which raced together for seven memorable seasons between the two world wars. Still regarded by many as the epitome of elegance under sail, these yachts were over 120' (36.5m) long, with low, graceful hulls that "overhung" the water by 20' (6m) at either end. Only ten of these craft were built, and all but one were intended to compete in the America's Cup. Their golden era was brought to an end by the start of World War II, but three of them survived and were subsequently restored and raced on the classic yacht circuit, where they still outclass all their rivals.

AFTER THE WAR

No one could afford the enormous overheads of the J-Class after the World War II, so the Deed of Gift was amended to allow the America's Cup to be raced on the more modest 12-meter (39') yachts. Although the boats were smaller, the racing was in many ways more exciting than before, with the yachts' close-quarters dueling and more teams competing to take part in the event.

America's 132-year stranglehold on the Cup—the longest winning streak in sporting history—was finally broken by the Australians in 1983, when *Australia II* came from behind in the last race to win by 41 seconds and take the series by 3–2.

RIGHT *The winged keel was a major innovation of the 1980s that was developed for the 12-meter* Australia II. *The vessel is shown here lifted clean out of the water.*

FAR RIGHT Endeavour *is one of only three original J-Class yachts still surviving. After a three-year refit at the Royal Huisman Shipyard in Holland, the yacht was once again afloat in July 1989.*

BOTTOM Australia II *beating upwind during Cowes Week 2000, Isle of Wight, UK.*

One of the greatest designers of the 12-meter (39') era was Olin Stephens, of the yacht design company Sparkman & Stephens. Between 1937 and 1980, Stephens designed the winning yachts for eight America's Cup challenges, including seven raced on 12-meters—beating the previous record held by Nathaniel Herreshoff, who designed or built all seven winners between 1893 and 1934.

The Americans won the Cup back in 1987, but it was back in court the following year when Michael Fay from New Zealand forced a challenge with a 90' (27m) sloop. In one of the Cup's all-time low points, the American's responded with a 60' (18m) catamaran and their own fleet of lawyers, winning the argument 2–0 on the water and, after a protracted battle, in the courtrooms, too.

THE MODERN ERA

The modern era of America's Cup racing was born in 1992, when the America's Cup Class was launched. A powerful yacht with a mainsail the size of a Boeing 747's wing, the new boats carried twice the sail area of their predecessors and looked about twice as appealing. Forever the ones to revel in a bit of style, the Italians put up some strong challenges in the new class, but it was Team New Zealand that snatched the Cup from the Americans in 1995 and put up a spirited defense to keep the Cup "down under" in 2000. It would take the might of a Swiss millionaire to wrench it off them and finally bring the Cup to Europe in 2003.

TOP *One of the most hotly contested silver cups in the world—the America's Cup—is held aloft by a victorious crew.*

SPECIFICATIONS OF THE BOATS

Enterprise, USA		*Shamrock V*, GB	
Length overall:	120' 9" (36.8m)	Length overall:	119' 1"(36.3m)
Length on waterline:	80' (24.4m)	Length on waterline:	81' 1" (24.7m)
Beam:	23' (7m)	Beam:	20' (6m)
Draft:	14' 6" (4.4m)	Draft:	14' 9"(4.5m)
Displacement:	128 tons (116,200kg)	Displacement:	134 tons (121,560kg)
Date launched:	1930	Date launched:	1930
Rainbow, USA		*Endeavour*, GB	
Length overall:	127' 6" (38.9m)	Length overall:	129' 6" (39.5m)
Length on waterline:	82' (25m)	Length on waterline:	83' 6" (25.4m)
Beam:	21' (6.4m)	Beam:	22' (6.7m)
Draft:	15' (4.6m)	Draft:	14' 9" (4.5m)
Displacement:	141 tons (127,900kg)	Displacement:	143 tons (129,730kg)
Date launched:	1934	Date launched:	1934

TOP *Team New Zealand drop their spinnaker during the 2007 America's Cup at Valencia, Spain— the first Cup to be held in Europe since 1851.*

TOP LEFT *The American and Italian teams battle it out for the Cup in 2007.*

LEFT *Alinghi beat Team New Zealand 5–2 to hang onto the Cup in 2007.*

Basic Folds & Rules for Racing

SEE TEMPLATES ON PAGES 41–48

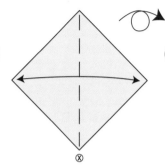

1 Start with the template, back side upward, rotated, so that the cross is lined up as shown. Crease and unfold a vertical diagonal.

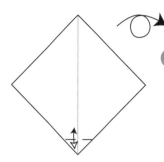

2 Turn the paper over. Crease and unfold a small corner upward.

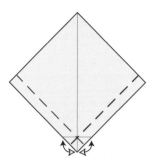

3 Turn the paper over. Fold two sides over to meet the recent crease, crease then unfold.

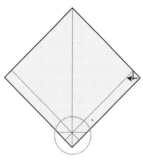

4 Fold the small corner over on the right. (The area in the circle is shown as an enlarged view in steps 5–7.)

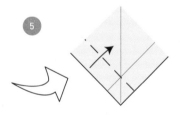

5 Fold the lower left edge over on the existing crease.

6 Tuck the triangular flap underneath.

7 Fold the lower right edge over, leaving the lower (white) corner flap where it is.

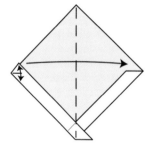

8 Fold the left-hand corner over, crease and unfold. Then fold in half from left to right.

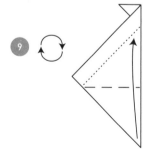

9 Rotate the paper 180°. Fold the lower corner to lie on a hidden edge, as shown.

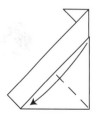

10 Fold the triangular flap in half.

11 Fold the new triangular flap in half, crease firmly, then unfold as shown.

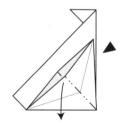

12 Open and squash the flap into a square.

The rules of America's Cup racing are famously complicated, but the end result is always the same: two boats fighting it out head to head on the water in a "first to five" (or "best of nine") series of races. The course consists of two 12-mile laps to a buoy laid to windward (the side facing the direction the wind is coming from). Careful preparation is essential. Our paper America's Cup yachts are based on the elegant J-Class icons of the 1930s and, like those boats, have a large sail area. We would therefore recommend adding a small coin by way of ballast on the windward side to prevent capsize. We would also advise scaling the course back to 12' (3.7m). A champagne cork tied to a pebble will make a suitable buoy. At the end of the series, why not sculpt a Cup from the cork wrapper and present it to the winner?

 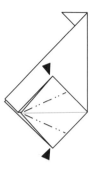 

13 Inside, reverse the corners.

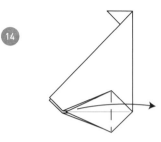

14 Fold the upper flap to the right.

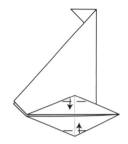

15 Fold the corners in about a third. The more you fold in, the slimmer your hull will become.

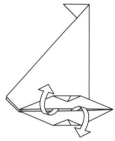

16 Hold the last step in place and very carefully, open the layers and wrap them around themselves. You will need to allow the paper to partially unfold, but try to keep the basic shape intact.

17 Here's the view from underneath when complete. Round the hull to make it more buoyant.

18 Fold over the tiny flap creased in step 8, tucking it behind a layer to hold the sail together.

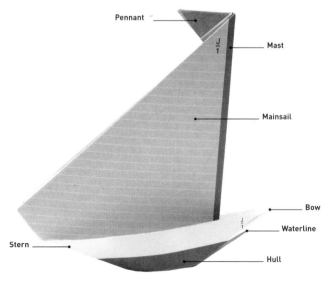

Pennant — Mast — Mainsail — Bow — Waterline — Hull — Stern

Complete!

Open 60

What is an Open 60? Most landlubbers have never heard of it, and many sailors only have a hazy notion of what it is. Yet most of us have probably seen one on the news without realizing it. When Tony Bullimore capsized in the Southern Ocean in 1997 and spent five days in his upside-down boat before being rescued by the Australian navy, he was sailing an Open 60. When Ellen McArthur finished second in the 2000–01 Vendée Globe round-the-world race on *Kingfisher*, she was also on an Open 60. And when British skipper Mike Golding rescued his rival Alex Thomson from his damaged yacht in the Southern Ocean in 2007, he too was sailing an Open 60.

Open 60s are super-lightweight sailboats designed to be controlled by one person. They are called "Open 60s" because they are 60' (18m) long and their design is "open" within certain constraints, such as minimum stability and safety requirements. This means that, unlike in a fixed design class, all the boats are slightly different. Built to race long distances across open oceans, usually without stopping, they have to strike a balance between being strong enough not to be pounded to pieces by storms and hurricanes, and yet be fast enough to be competitive.

The yachts' hulls are usually built out of carbon fiber, with towering carbon fiber masts, vast Kevlar sails, and a deep bulb keel to keep it all upright. They are fitted with every electronic gismo for navigation, weather forecasting, and satellite communications. However, the living quarters are extremely modest and usually limited to a 21.5ft^2 (2m^2) "bubble" in the middle of the boat, where the skippers have to eat, sleep, and navigate. This is no luxury cruise.

THE FIRST OPEN 60

The first official Open 60 was *Thursday's Child*, built in 1983 for Warren Luhrs, the boss of a well-known British boatbuilding company called Hunter Marine. She was the first modern yacht to be specifically designed for long-distance, single-handed sailing and was fitted with a number of innovations, such as water ballast and a pendulum rudder. The yacht made an immediate impact, winning the 1984 single-handed transatlantic race and setting a new record for the course. Five years later, she became the first boat to break the New York to San Francisco sailing record that had been set by the clipper ship *Flying Cloud* in 1853.

DEVELOPING THE CONCEPT

The Open 60 concept was taken a step further by French designers Groupe Finot. For the 1989–90 Vendée Globe round-the-world race, they produced what was generally regarded as a beast of a machine. *Generali Concorde*, named after her sponsors, was far wider and flatter than any other boat in the race, and drew comparisons with a giant windsurfer. Her designers had realized that, since most of the race was sailed downwind (following the prevailing winds and currents going around the globe from west to east), what was needed was a big, wide platform, stable enough to surf down the monster Southern Ocean waves for literally weeks at a time.

TOP *A jubilant Kojiro Shiraishi on* Spirit of Yukoh *takes second place overall in the Velux 5 Oceans single-handed round-the-world race in 2006–07, achieving the highest-ever position for a Japanese solo sailor in the Open 60 class.*

TOP *The fleet assemble in Bilbao port,at the start of the 2006–07 Velux 5 Oceans single-handed round-the-world race.*

TOP LEFT Veolia Environnement *is one of the more advanced Open 60s, which are fitted with rotating masts.*

BOTTOM LEFT Cheminées Poujoulat *faces 70-knot winds in the notorious Bay of Biscay at the start of the 2006–07 Velux 5 Oceans solo round-the-world yacht race.*

BOTTOM RIGHT *A modern Open 60 with a distinctive wedge shape takes part in the 2008 Artemis Transat from Plymouth (UK) to Boston (USA).*

Although *Generali Concorde* did not fare particularly well in that race, mainly due to technical problems, she placed second in the BOC round-the-world race two years later—only beaten by the even more extreme *Groupe Sceta*, also designed by Groupe Finot. The trend had been set, and from then on the major single-handed races would become increasingly dominated by the Open 60 class. So much so that, from 2004, they were the only boats allowed to compete in the Vendée Globe—a race generally regarded as the "Everest" of sailing.

REGULATION

In 1991, the class created its own governing body, the International 60ft Monohull Open Class Association (IMOCA), which regulates the boats' design and construction rules, and runs the racing calendar. As other classes have waned, the Open 60 has attracted increasing numbers of sponsors and its race calendar has expanded accordingly. Some thirty-two boats took part in the 2008 championship, and the class officially takes part in eight major events, including two round-the-world and four transatlantic races.

NEW GENERATION

The new generation of boats unveiled for the 2008–09 Vendée Globe makes those early Open 60s seem positively conservative. *Pindar*, designed by Volvo Ocean Race designer Juan Kouyoumdjian, is 21' (6.4m) wide with a 99' (30m) tall mast, making her the most powerful boat in the fleet. That means that she'll perform well in light airs, but once she gets on the Southern Ocean "merry-go-round," her skipper Brian Thomson might regret all that windage aloft. After all, ocean racing is not only about speed, it is also about not breaking your boat.

Ecover, by comparison, is relatively moderate, at 19' (5.8m) wide and sporting an 88' 6" (27m) mast. Her skipper, Mike Golding, knows all about ocean sailing. A former professional firefighter, he has sailed around the world five times (including two previous Vendée Globes) and in the process has at various times been dismasted, lost a keel, and run aground. This time he has chosen the safer option knowing that if he can keep his boat together, he has the cunning to outwit his rivals.

By contrast, Alex Thomson on *Hugo Boss* is famous for pushing hard and sailing fast. That is why he holds the single-handed monohull 24-hour speed record—it may also be why he had to pull out of the last two round-the-world races due to boat damage. His new *Hugo Boss* has several innovative features, including "angled" bilges, rather than the usual round ones, and steering positions on both sides of the boat, rather than a single central steering "pod."

Alex Thomson made headlines around the world in 2006 when he had to abandon ship in the Southern Ocean while competing in the Velux 5 Oceans single-handed round-the-world race. The British sailor was in third place on *Hugo Boss*, sailing 1,000 miles south of Cape Town, South Africa, when

TOP Hugo Boss *is a new generation Open 60 launched in 2008 for the Vendée Globe race. Her predecessor had to be abandoned in the Southern Ocean in 2006.*

TOP *Mike Golding and his Ecover yachts have achieved a podium place in all the top solo races for the past ten years.*

RIGHT *Safran's extremely wide "rear end" is typical of all modern Open 60s.*

FAR RIGHT *PRB, winner of the last two Vendée Globe races, is one of the fleet of paper yachts represented at the back of this book.*

TOP Pakea *on the second leg of the 2006–07 Velux 5 Oceans race from Fremantle, Australia, to Norfolk, Virginia, USA. Its skipper, Unai Basurko goes on to finish in third place, becoming the first Spaniard to reach the winner's poduim in a round-the-world race.*

the keel of the yacht suffered "extreme structural failure." Mike Golding, with whom Thomson had a long-standing feud, was in second place and had to sail back 80 miles against strong winds and heavy seas to rescue his fellow competitor. Less than six hours later, the mast on Golding's own yacht (*Ecover*) collapsed and the two former enemies were forced to sail back to Cape Town under jury rig. After touring TV and radio studios to tell their story, the pair ended up the best of friends.

GOING FOR A HAT TRICK

The other two Open 60s in our little group are *PRB* and *Artemis*. The first few yachts launched by sponsors PRB suffered a string of disasters with French sailor Isabelle Autissier at the helm, including two sinkings and a retirement in three consecutive races. The brand has come into its own recently, however, winning the last two editions of the Vendée Globe, most recently in 2005 with current skipper Vincent Riou at the helm. Not surprisingly, the yacht was among the favorites to win the next race, starting from Les Sables d'Olonnes in France in November 2008, to clinch a hat trick.

Artemis, by comparison, is a relative newcomer to ocean racing and entered the Vendée Globe for the first time in 2008, with rookie skipper Jonny Malbon in charge. Judging from Malbon's previous result—including breaking the Round Britain and Ireland record in 2006 on *Artemis's* previous Open 60—he stood every chance of pulling a surprise out of the hat.

SPECIFICATIONS OF THE BOATS

Ecover		*Hugo Boss*	
Length:	60' (18.3m)	Length:	60' (18.3m)
Beam:	19' (5.8m)	Beam:	17' 2" (5.2m)
Draft:	14' 9" (4.5m)	Draft:	14' 9" (4.5m)
Displacement:	9 tons (8,164kg)	Displacement:	9 tons (8,164kg)
Mast height:	88' 6" (27m)	Mast height:	88' 6" (27m)
Upwind sail area:	3,229ft^2 (300m^2)	Upwind sail area:	3,229ft^2 (300m^2)
Downwind sail area:	6,243ft^2 (580m^2)	Downwind sail area:	5,920ft^2 (550m^2)
PRB		*Artemis*	
Length:	60' (18.3m)	Length:	60' (18.3m)
Beam:	19' 2" (5.85m)	Beam:	20' (6m)
Draft:	14' 9" (4.5m)	Draft:	14' 9" (4.5m)
Displacement:	9 tons (8,164kg)	Displacement:	9 tons (8,164kg)
Mast height:	88' 6" (27m)	Mast height:	91' 8" (28m)
Upwind sail area:	3,229ft^2 (300m^2)	Upwind sail area:	3,767ft^2 (350m^2)
Downwind sail area:	5,381ft^2 (500m^2)	Downwind sail area:	6,458ft^2 (600m^2)

LEFT *Alex Thomson's Hugo Boss weathers a force 10 gale on the second day of the single-handed round-the-world 2006–07 race.*

FAR LEFT *Jubilant Open 60 competitors celebrate their return home after spending more than three months at sea.*

BOTTOM *The start of the 2006–07 Velux 5 Oceans race in Bilbao. Only four of the seven starters managed to complete the 30,000-mile course.*

Basic Folds & Rules for Racing

SEE TEMPLATES ON PAGES 49–56

1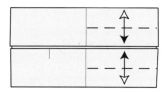

Start with the square template, back side upward, so that the cross is lined up as shown. Fold in half both ways, then open back to the square.

2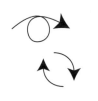

Fold the lower left corner to the center, make a small pinch, then unfold.

3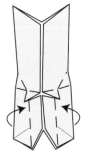

Fold upper and lower edges to the horizontal center crease.

4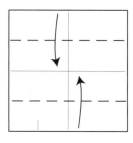

In the right-hand section only, fold upper and lower edges to the horizontal center, crease and unfold.

5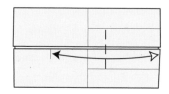

Fold the right center to meet the pinchmark, only creasing in the central section. Unfold again.

6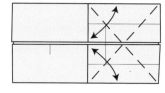

Add diagonal creases on the right side.

7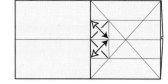

Turn the paper over. Make two small diagonal creases, then turn the paper back over.

8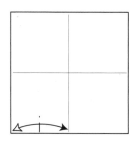

Rotate to this position. Start to put the creases shown into the paper, forming it into three dimensions.

9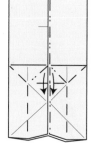

This is the move in progress. Flatten the paper.

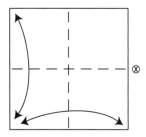

Open 60s are designed for long passages out in the open sea, and it will be tempting, once the paper yacht is built, to put her on the water and watch her sail over the horizon. Try to restrain yourself from doing this—at least until you've had a few races. This is the most compact of our paper racers and, suitably ballasted with a couple of small coins placed on the windward side, she should withstand a bit more wind that our flighty America's Cup yacht. The Vendée Globe, the ultimate Open 60 race, is a 26,000-mile non-stop thrash around the world, past the Cape of Good Hope, Cape Leeuwin and Cape Horn. Find a suitably circular water course to sail, line up three buoys to replicate the Capes and let your paper yachts loose. Remember, no short-tacking or stopping off en route unless it is written in the rules. This is serious racing!

10 Fold in the left-hand short edges on both sides.

11 Fold the upper layer to the left, crease and return (note that the lower end of the crease is slightly above the bottom corner).

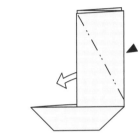

12 Inside, reverse the same corner using the crease you've just made.

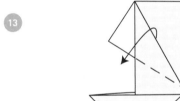

13 Unfold the sail fully.

14 Fold the upper edge to meet the edge of the sail.

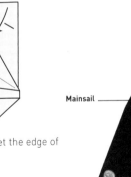

15 Now fold the same flap over again, tucking it underneath the sail.

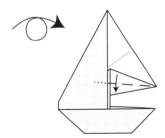

16 Turn the paper over. Fold the colored flap in half, making the sail fully white.

Complete!

Mast / Mainsail / GBR 100 / ARTEMIS / ARTEMIS OCEAN RACING / Jib / Stern / ARTEMIS 100 / Bow / Hull

Volvo Open 70

It's a grueling prospect by any standard: 37,000 miles of sailing over nine months; eight crews racing each other around the world in ten legs, with no let-up no matter what the weather. And the risks are very real. Three people died during the inaugural event in 2005–06, and two more died in subsequent races. No wonder the Volvo Ocean Race is known as one of the toughest sporting events on the planet.

The boats that have evolved to cope with such a challenge are a unique breed. They need to be tough enough to take whatever the ocean will throw at them. They also have to accommodate eleven crew members and all the food and gear needed to keep them going for up to five weeks at a time. They also have to be very fast.

THE FIRST VOLVO OPEN 70S

The formula for the first wave of Volvo Open 70s (VO70s) was essentially a scaled-up version of the Open 60s, with enormously wide, flat-bottomed hulls designed to ride the Southern Ocean waves. Problems with the new design soon became apparent, however, with several boats in the 2005–06 edition of the race suffering from keel failure. Two teams had to have their boats shipped out for the second leg of the race, while the Spanish entry *Movistar* was abandoned mid-Atlantic on the fourth leg.

THE NEW GENERATION

For the 2008–09 edition of the race, the route was changed, controversially, so that the fleet sailed further north, stopping off in India, Singapore, and China, before heading briefly south to round Cape Horn and sail up to North America. As a result, the new generation of VO70s were designed with upwind performance in mind—and with sail wardrobes to match. New rules were drawn up to ban the problematic keels and also to allow the boats to be fitted with modern, lightweight rigging.

The resulting yacht is a battle-hardened workhorse, designed to race at sustained speeds of up to 40 knots. It is certainly exciting to sail but it is not very comfortable for the crew.

It is all a long way from the very first Whitbread round-the-world race, as the event was originally called. A mixed fleet of seventeen boats lined up for the start of the inaugural race in 1974, ranging from production yachts to specially-designed ocean racers. There were just four stops in the 27,500-mile course, which started and finished in Portsmouth, England, and circled the world via the "three capes:" the Cape of Good Hope, Chile, Cape Leeuwin in Australia, and Cape Horn, South Africa. The second leg, between Cape Town and Sydney, turned out to be the most deadly, with the British, French, and Italian teams each losing a crew member over the side. The extreme weather conditions meant it was impossible to turn around in time to pick the person up alive.

TOP *Swedish team's Assa Abloy is an example of the old style 60-footers (18m). These boats were still in use when the Whitbread round-the-world race was renamed the Volvo Ocean Race in 2001–02.*

LEFT Assa Abloy *crashes through a wave at 30 knots on the second leg of the 2001–02 race.*

BOTTOM LEFT Amer Sport One *broaches out of control on the approach to Australia, the second and most perilous leg.*

BOTTOM *Temporarily into calmer waters,* Team Tyco *crosses the Caribbean on leg five of the 2001–02 race.*

In the end, it was one of the smaller boats in the fleet, the 65' (19.8m) Mexican yacht *Sayula*, that won the race overall, in 152 days.

It wasn't until the sixth edition that the organizers decided to design a yacht specifically for the event. By then, the gap between the big, no-holds-barred maxi-yachts and the rest of the fleet was so big that some of the smaller boats were finishing ten days behind the winner on each leg—or up to fifty-two days behind on aggregate time. The Whitbread 60 was introduced in 1993–94, racing alongside the maxis for the first race before the maxis were banned altogether in 1997–98. American sailor Paul Cayard won the first all-W60 race, skippering the Swedish entry *EF Language*.

TOP Green Dragon *heads off from Alicante, Spain, on the first leg of the 2008–09 race—next stop 6,500 miles to Cape Town, South Africa.*

VOLVO AS SPONSORS

By the time Volvo took over as title sponsors in 2001, the event had grown to 32,700 miles and ten legs, including two stops in North America: Miami and Baltimore. The number of entries, however, was down to just eight teams, almost entirely composed of ocean-hardened professionals. Indeed, the race had by then become a seal of success for many up-and-coming young sailors. Its impressive alumni included stars such as France's Eric Tabarly and the UK's Chay Blyth in the early days, through to the USA's Dennis Conner and New Zealand's Peter Blake. Later stars included Paul Cayard and Grant Dalton. Even the plucky Tracy Edwards had her moment in the sun when she put together her all-girl crew on *Maiden* in 1989–90—many of whom would go on to become successful racers in their own right.

MAKING RECORDS

Yacht design had moved on considerably by the mid-2000s, thanks to the cutting-edge Open 60 designs that were dominating the single-handed circuit. The old Whitbread 60 (now the Volvo 60) was looking increasingly outdated and was duly replaced in the 2005–06 by the Volvo Open 70, which was some 6.5' (2m) longer and one metric ton (1,000kg) lighter than its predecessor. Clearly inspired by the now well-established Open 60 class, the new boat had the wide, flat surfing hull of its smaller cousin—which had proven so effective in the Southern Ocean—as well as the distinctive wedge-shape when seen from above. It carried up to 60 percent more sail and allowed the use of canting keels, something which would lead to most of the "teething" problems encountered in its first outing.

The new boats soon vindicated themselves by breaking the world 24-hour monohull record three times during the course of the race, finishing with the 23.45-knot record set by *ABN AMRO 2*, which still stands. Competition between the teams was so close that, after sailing all the way from Australia to New Zealand, the leading boats on the third leg were just nine seconds apart. There was triumph and tragedy for the two Dutch teams, with *ABN AMRO 1* winning in emphatic style with Mike Sanderson at the helm, while on *ABN AMRO 2*, crew member Hans Horrevoets had fallen over the side and drowned in the Atlantic.

LEFT *The all-new Volvo 70 class* Ericsson *in pre-race testing off the coast of Spain in 2005.*

BOTTOM LEFT *The second-generation Volvo 70s line up in Alicante's Race Village Marina, Spain, in 2008.*

BOTTOM RIGHT *Team Russia on board their Volvo 70 yacht* Kosatka. *The name means "killer whale" in Russian.*

BOTTOM *In-port practice racing in Alicante, Portugal at the start of the 2008–09 race.*

TOP Green Dragon, *one of the early winners in 2008–09, but maintaining consistent form over the nine months of the race is the key to success.*

There were other innovations in the 2005–06 race, including in-port racing at most of the stopovers, using the exciting new catamaran class, the Extreme 40s (see pages 32–9). The idea was to attract bigger audiences during the stopovers and, with 2.8 million visitors recorded during the entire event, the plan seems to have succeeded. It was also the first edition of the race not to start from England, foreshadowing the complete break with the mother country in 2008–09 when, for the first time, none of the stops would take place in the UK.

There was uproar in the yachting world when the organizers announced that the 2008–09 edition of the race would eschew the time-honored Southern Ocean route in favor of a more coastal route. Starting in October 2008, the fleet sailed up the Indian Ocean to Cochin in India and on to Singapore and then Qingdao in China, before rounding Cape Horn to Boston, USA, and finishing in St. Petersburg, Russia, in June 2009. But while the new course meant the competitors no longer had to slalom through the icebergs of the far south, their journey was in other ways every bit as challenging—and considerably longer—than the original route.

PREDICTING THE OUTCOME

With so many changes, the winner of the 2008–09 edition was never going to be easy to predict. The double entries from *Telefónica* and *Ericsson* were the experts' favorites before the start, but with *Telefónica Blue* suffering damage in the early stages and *Green Dragon* putting on a stronger-than-expected performance, the race was wide open. As Shaun Carkeek and Marcelino Botin, designers of the American entry *Puma*, said: "It's hard to anticipate how things are going to unfold. I think the sailing conditions are very different on each leg and therefore some boats will be better in some stages and worse in others. We may find that the best all-round boat is not the best boat in any of the legs. This is certainly the case in some of the computer models that we were running and it could turn out to be the case in the actual race. So I would say the team needs to be patient and consistent and aim at getting good overall results in all the different stages of the race."

SPECIFICATIONS OF THE BOATS (ALL YACHTS IDENTICAL)	
Length overall:	70' 6" (21.5m)
Beam:	16' 5"–18' 6" (5–5.6m)
Draft:	14' 6" (4.4m)
Mast height:	103' 4" (31.5m)
Weight:	Approx. 15 tons (13,000–13,608kg)
Keel weight:	Approx. 6–8 tons (5,443–7,257kg)
Sail area upwind:	2,895ft² (269m²)
Sail area downwind:	7,265ft² (675m²)

TOP *The 2008–09 fleet leaves Alicante, Spain, at the start of the 37,000-mile race.*

TOP LEFT *The Russian team break away from the start line. In shape, these modern Volvo yachts are similar to the Open 60s, except they are 10ft (3m) longer.*

BOTTOM LEFT *Telefonica Blue, one of the early favorites to win the 2008–09 race, makes an unscheduled stop to repair a broken rudder only one day into the race.*

BOTTOM RIGHT *Sailing around the world on a Volvo 70 is hard, wet work—and also completely exhilarating.*

Basic Folds & Rules for Racing

SEE TEMPLATES ON PAGES 57–64

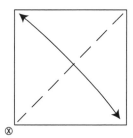

1 Start with the square template, front side upward, so that the cross is lined up as shown. Crease and unfold a diagonal.

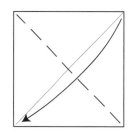

2 Fold the top right corner to the bottom left.

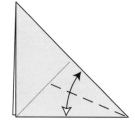

3 Fold the lower first edge to the folded edge, crease only as far as the diagonal crease, then unfold.

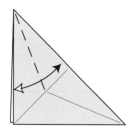

4 This is the result. Repeat the fold on the other half of the paper.

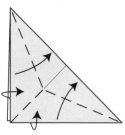

5 Fold left and lower edges over on the crease you have just made. Form a triangular flap that points upwards.

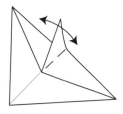

6 Flatten the flap both ways, leave it folded away from you.

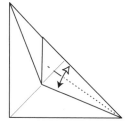

7 Fold the first layer of the outer edge to meet the inner folded edge. Make a tiny pinch mark through the diagonal crease.

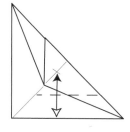

8 Fold the lower edge to where the diagonal and pinch creases meet. Do not crease on the left of the diagonal crease. Unfold. Decreasing this distance, and in step 9, will make the hull shallower.

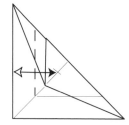

9 Repeat the move on the opposite side.

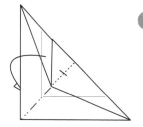

10 Fold the upper half of the paper behind. Check the next drawing for guidance.

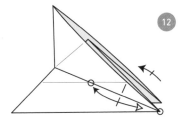

11 Fold the corner to the circled point, crease firmly and unfold. Repeat on the other side.

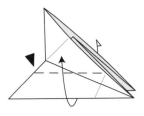

12 Open up the lower layers on either side, wrapping them up and around the sail.

Our paper Volvo Open 70 is the most rugged design of the collection. After all, if we're going long-distance sailing with a big crew, the priority is to stay dry and upright. Ballasting with a small coin or two is again key—this time with the coins placed in the bow (front) of the boat to counteract the structural weight in the stern (back). The Volvo 70s stop off several times as they sail around the world. The 2008–09 course was made up of ten legs, each averaging 3,700 miles. This may be ambitious for our models, but they might reasonably sail ten 12' (3.7m) legs, with the wind behind them. Ask ten friends to stand 12' apart, around the edge of a pond. They can collect the boats as they finish and relay them to the next person. If your group is very competitive, use a stopwatch and add together the times for each leg to find the overall winner.

 13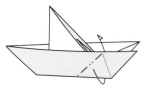

Wrap the coloured layer inside and upwards, on an existing crease.

14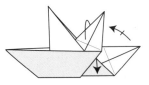

Like this. Unfold it and repeat on the other side.

15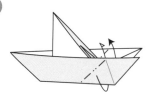

Now refold both sides, overlapping them.

 16

Fold the stern layers over, tucking them inside. Plump the sail out slightly to finish the design.

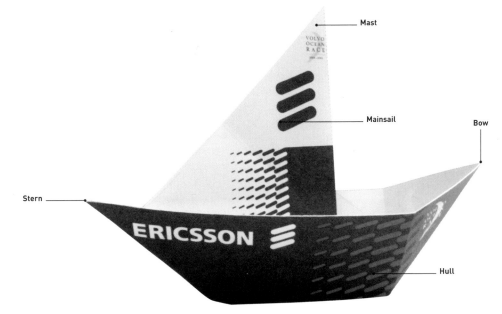

Mast

Mainsail

Bow

Stern

Hull

Complete!

The Extreme 40 was conceived by and born into a family of the hardiest sailors on the planet. Originally devised to provide inshore racing during the stopovers of the 2005–06 Volvo Ocean Race, the class has quickly become a firm favorite among crews from the America's Cup, the Olympics, and the Volvo Ocean Race itself. It is as if the elite of the yachting world conspired to produce the most exhilarating, out-and-out racing machine they could—and came up with the Extreme 40.

In 1976 the first catamaran was accepted as an Olympic class. The concept soon caught on, and the 20' (6m) Tornado is now raced all over the world. Among its proponents were Yves Loday (Olympic Gold medal, 1992), Mitch Booth (Bronze 1992, Silver 1996) and Herbert Dercksen (three-time winner of the Catamaran World Championships), who were instrumental in the creation and promotion of the Extreme 40 class. The design they came up with has similarities with the Tornado, albeit stretched to 40' (12.2m).

Like the Tornado, the Extreme 40 has a pair of slender, wave-piercing hulls, with a simple trapeze stretched between them, and no sleeping quarters. To keep the boat as light as possible, the hulls are built from carbon fiber with a Nomex core. The boat is capable of speeds of up to 40 knots and are billed as the "fastest 40' yacht in the world." In keeping with its intended role of traveling the globe, the Extreme 40 dismantles and can be packed into a standard container and loaded on the back of a truck or container ship. Once unloaded, it takes about six hours to put back together and weighs just over one metric ton (1,250kg). It retails for around one-sixth the price of an Open 60.

The Extreme 40 provides a thrilling ride for the four crew and fifth person (usually owner, sponsor, or journalist), since much of the racing is done with one hull out of the water, known as "flying." Round-the-world yachtsman Nigel King says: "Sailing isn't like other training, a marathon or a triathlon, it's mega-explosive. You have to make your heart and lungs work very hard or you're not actually training for your sport. You have to put yourself under pressure for that sudden explosive burst, then recover briefly, then put yourself back under pressure again."

THE FIRST EXTREME 40S

Five Extreme 40s were built for the 2005–06 Volvo Ocean Race and wowed spectators and crews alike at the race stopovers in Spain, Rio de Janeiro, Baltimore, Portsmouth, and Rotterdam. Consistently at the front of the fleet was two-time Olympic medalist Randy Smyth on *Tommy Hilfiger*, with solo round-the-world yachtsman Conrad Humphries on *Motorola-CHR* snapping at his heels. Record-breaking yachtswoman Dee Caffari described the boats as "one huge blast."

The following year, with no Volvo Ocean Race to shadow, the iShares Cup was created specially for the class. Operated by Offshore Challenges, the company co-owned by British yachtswoman Dame Ellen MacArthur, four more boats were built, and the nine teams raced at venues all around Europe.

ABOVE *Extreme 40 crews can "fly" a hull in very light winds, providing an exhilarating ride onboard. The races are sailed in inshore waters by four crew and a "fifth man" (or woman)—often a media representative or team sponsor.*

LEFT *Members of Oman's elite military forces sail the Sultan's Extreme 40.*

FAR BOTTOM *The 2008 iShares Cup finals in Amsterdam, Holland.*

BOTTOM *The Extreme 40s' ultra-light hulls are made from carbon fiber using Formula 1 technology.*

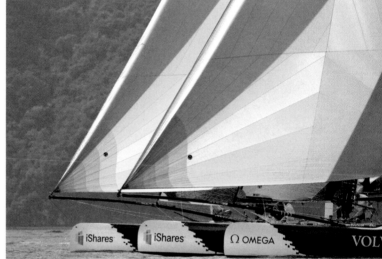

Four of the boats even showed up for the Round the Island—the legendary race around the Isle of Wight—where Dame Ellen beat all comers to take line honors on *JP Morgan Asset Management*. In the final race of the iShares series in Amsterdam, however, it was the turn of *Basilica*, skippered by Volvo Ocean Race veteran Rob Greenhalgh, to claim victory.

The series was repeated in 2008, this time with ten boats, including two America's Cup teams: current Cup holders *Alinghi*, from Switzerland, and Britain's aspiring challengers *TeamOrigin*. The Cup teams certainly brought an extra degree of competition (and glamor) to the racing, bringing with them some big names, such as two-time Cup winner Ed Baird (*Alinghi*, skipper), Volvo Ocean Race winner Mike Sanderson (*TeamOrigin*, Team Director) and two-time Olympic Gold medalist Shirley Robertson (*JP Morgan*, Skipper).

With no America's Cup challenge in 2008, the two Cup teams dominated the Extreme 40 circuit that year. *TeamOrigin* gave a consistent performance, coming second in the first four rounds and heading the leaderboard for most of the year. *Alinghi*, by contrast, started badly on their home turf in Switzerland, but won the next three rounds. They finished the season neck-and-neck and although skipper Rob Greenhalgh looked like making it two in a row, the British team struggled in the last round at Amsterdam and, in the very final race, conceded the series to *Alinghi*.

TOP *Extreme 40s in action during the UK leg of the iShares Cup 2008 series.*

CLASS OF THE FUTURE

With some of the world's top sailors taking part, the racing in 2008 was even more competitive than before—as testified by the seven capsizes in the seventy seven races of the series. With the 2008–09 edition of the Volvo Ocean Race kicking off in October 2008, the Extreme 40s went back to their original role— that of providing in-port racing during five of the ten stopovers, in Alicante, Singapore, Qingdao, Boston, and Stockholm. They are increasingly becoming the race boats of the future.

SPECIFICATIONS OF THE BOATS (ALL YACHTS IDENTICAL)

Length overall:	40' (12.2m)
Beam:	26' (7.9m)
Displacement:	1 ton (907kg)
Mast height:	62' (18.9m)
Mainsail:	807ft² (75m²) (upwind & downwind sailing)
Jib:	269ft² (25m²) (upwind sailing)
Gennaker:	839ft² (78m²) (downwind sailing)
Top speed:	40 knots

LEFT *One of the America's Cup teams taking part in 2008 are the current Cup holders Alinghi.*

FAR LEFT *The US* Tommy Hilfiger *sailing team under pressure in the second leg of the 2007 iShares Cup series, held in Marseille, France.*

BOTTOM *Team yachts congregate for some in-port racing during one of the stopovers of the iShares Cup 2008 series.*

Basic Folds & Rules for Racing

Hull

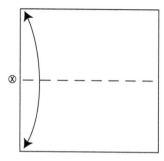

1 Start with the square template, back side upward. Fold in half vertically, then unfold.

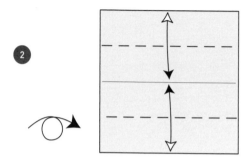

2 Turn the paper over. Fold the outer edges to the center, crease and unfold.

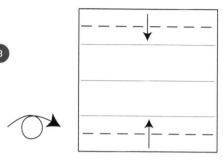

3 Turn the paper over. Fold upper and lower edges to the quarter creases.

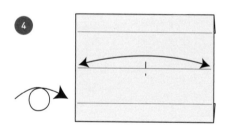

4 Turn over once more. Gently mark the center of the central horizontal crease.

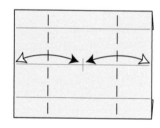

5 Fold left and right edges to the center, crease and unfold.

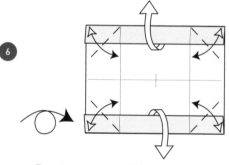

6 Turn the paper over. Fold all corners to meet the nearest vertical crease, then unfold back to the square.

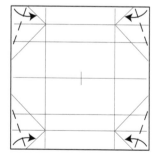

7 Fold the corners in to lie on the angled creases (see the next drawing).

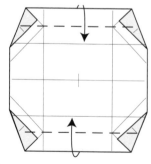

8 Refold on the outer eighth creases.

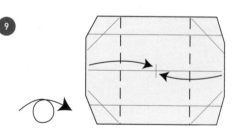

9 Turn the paper over. Fold left and right sides to the center.

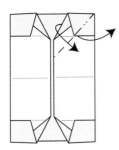

10 Pull out the upper right corner, flattening on existing creases.

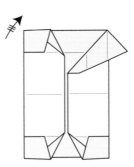

11 This is how the top right corner should look. Repeat on the three other corners.

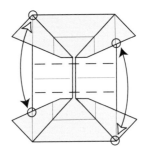

12 Fold the circled corners to meet, making sharp horizontal creases.

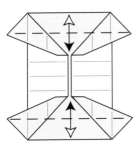

13 Refold the creases shown, to pass them through the upper layers.

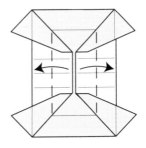

14 Fold the inner white edges to the outer vertical edges.

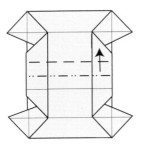

15 Form a pleat using existing creases.

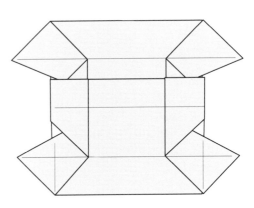

The hull is complete.

Sail

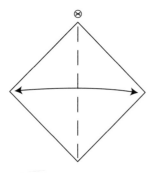

1 Start with the square template, back side upward, rotated, so that the cross is lined up as shown. Crease and unfold a vertical diagonal.

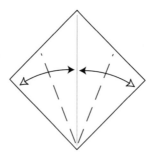

2 Fold both lower edges to the vertical center. Crease, and unfold.

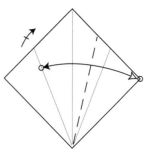

3 Fold the lower left edge to lie along the crease on the opposite side (the circled points meet), then unfold. Repeat on the opposite side.

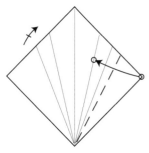

4 Fold the lower left edge to the most recent crease. Repeat on the other side.

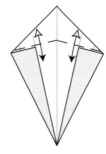

5 Fold both upper edges over the folded edge, crease as far as the vertical center, then unfold.

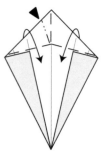

6 Fold both sides in together, flattening the center flap to the left, forming a new mountain crease.

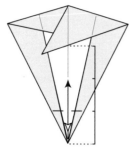

7 Fold the lower corner over, roughly one-third of the distance shown. Crease and unfold.

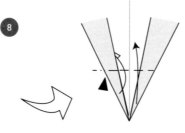

8 An enlarged view of the lower corner. Fold the right side over normally, on the left, fold the paper inside (see next drawing).

9 Fold the paper in half from left to right, tucking the flap on the left into a pocket on the right. The sail is now complete.

Extreme 40 racing is fast and exciting. Courses must be kept short with a maximum possibility of capsize. Ballasting the paper yachts to take into account the prevailing breeze is an important consideration and may be done using coins of different sizes and weights placed in the windward hull. With all the yachts correctly ballasted, they can then be lined up and the race can begin. Once the vessels are released, no contact may be made between competitor and vessel other than to change tack (alter direction through a minimum of 90°). Competitors may, however, use their own breath to encourage their craft onto the correct course, particularly if a collision or shipwreck is imminent. Competitors are not allowed to blow competing yachts off course, although in certain exceptional circumstances some "foul air" from rival vessels is only to be expected. In keeping with the full-size Extreme 40 circuit, three to five windward/leeward races should be raced in total and, as no protests are allowed, the "first-past-the-post" system applies.

Assembly

1 Arrange the hull and sail as shown. Slide the sail under the hull, tucking the corners into the pleat made in step 15 of the hull.

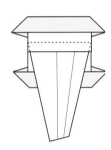

2 This is the result. Turn the paper over.

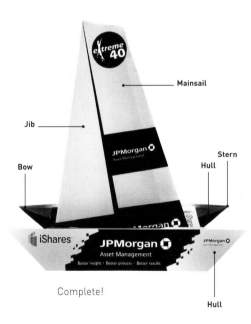

Jib Mainsail Bow Stern Hull

Complete!

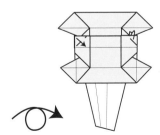

3 Fold one corner of the pleat towards you, the other away from you, to "lock" the sail into the hull.

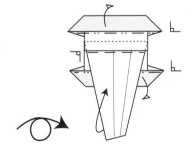

4 Turn back over. Fold the sides of the hull down at 90°and arrange the sail vertically.

Glossary & Resources

GLOSSARY OF YACHTING TERMS

ballast—Weight, usually in the form of heavy metal such as lead, placed in the lowest part of the boat to increase its stability.

beam—The width of a boat at its widest point.

bilge—The lowest part of the inside of a boat, usually under the cabin sole.

bow—The front, or "pointy" end, of a boat (though note that some boats can be "pointy" at both ends!)

canting keel—A keel (see below) that can be adjusted to optimize its angle to the hull.

catamaran—A vessel with two parallel hulls joined by crossbars.

change tack—To alter the boat's direction so that the wind moves from one side of the sails to the other.

clipper ship—Large sailing ship used to carry cargo in the nineteenth century, especially tea from China to Europe.

displacement—The weight of a boat, as measured by the weight of water it displaces when floating.

downwind—In the direction the wind is blowing towards.

draft—The depth of a boat at its deepest point.

gennaker—A large sail set forward of the mast—halfway between a "genoa" and a "spinnaker."

genoa—A large sail—set forward of the mast—which overlaps the mainsail.

hull—The main body of a boat.

jib—A small triangular sail set forward of the mast.

keel—The lowest part of the hull, which prevents a sailboat sliding across the water when the sails are pressed by the wind.

knot—A unit of measure for the speed of a boat, equivalent to 1.15mph.

leeward—The direction or side of the boat away from the wind.

mainsail—A large (usually triangular) sail set behind and attached to the mast.

mast—A large vertical pole to which the sails are attached.

match racing—A race between only two boats at a time.

nautical mile—Unit of measurement equivalent to 1.15 statute (land) mile.

pennant—nautical flag tapering to a point, used for identification or signalling.

port—The side of a boat on the left when facing forward.

rigging—The ropes and wires used to secure the mast and sails.

schooner—A sailboat with at least two masts of equal height, or with the mast nearer the stern (back) being the taller.

short-tacking—Sailing a course that needs frequent changes of tack (i.e. direction).

single-handed—Sailing with just one person on board.

sloop—A sailboat with one mast, setting only one sail forward of the mast.

spinnaker—A large, balloon-like sail set forward of the mast.

starboard—The side of a boat on the right when facing forward.

starboard tack—Sailing with the wind on the right-hand side of the boat. Sailboats sailing on starboard tack have priority over sailboats sailing on the port tack (i.e. with the wind blowing on the left-hand side).

stern—The back, or "blunt" end, of a boat (some boats can be "pointy" at both ends).

tacking—Sailing with the wind on the forward side of the boat, with the aim of making progress in the direction from which the wind is coming.

trapeze—A harness attached to a wire attached to the mast, used to hold a crew leaning out of a small boat to create extra leverage to prevent the boat from capsizing.

upwind—In or toward the direction from which the wind is coming.

windward—In the direction from which the wind is coming. Against the wind.

RESOURCES

A.C. Moore
Corporate Office
130 A.C. Moore Drive,
Berlin, NJ 08009
1-888-ACMOORE OPTION-2
www.acmoore.com
• Arts and crafts suppliers with stores across the USA. See website for store locations.

Dick Blick
P.O. Box 1267
Galesburg, IL 61402-1267
1-800-828-4548
www.dickblick.com
• Art materials suppliers. Products can be ordered online or purchased in store. See website for store locations.

Graphic Products Corporation
455 Maple Ave.
Carpenterville, IL 60110
1-847-836-9600
www.gpcpapers.com
• Supplier of graphic arts products. Products are available to order online and at various stores across America. See website for store locations.

Hiromi Paper International
2525 Michigan Ave., Unit G-9
Santa Monica, CA 90404
1-866-479-2744
www.hiromipaper.com
• Supplier of Japanese paper. Products are available to order online. See website for details.

Jo-Ann
Corporate Office
5555 Darrow Rd.
Hudson, OH 44236
1-888-739-4120
www.joann.com
• Supplier of fabric and craft products. Order online or see website for store locations.

Kelly Paper
Corporate Office
288 Brea Canyon Rd.
City of Industry, CA 91789
1-800-675-3559
www.kellypaper.com
• Wholesale paper supplier. Products can be ordered online or purchased in store. See website for store locations.

Legion Paper
11 Madison Ave.
New York, NY 10010
1-800-278-4478
(International): (212) 683-6990
www.legionpaper.com
• Supplier of fine art paper. Order online or see website for store locations.

Michaels Stores, Inc.
8000 Bent Branch Dr.
Irving, TX 75063
1-800-642-4235
www.michaels.com
• Arts and crafts suppliers with stores across the USA. Products can be viewed online, but are only available for purchase in store. See website for store locations.

Origami USA
15 West 77 Street
New York, NY 10024-5192
1-212-769-5635
www.origami-usa.org
• Website devoted to origami, offering many resources for origami aficionados.

Pearl
1033 E. Oakland Park Blvd.
Fort Lauderdale,
FL 33334
1-800-451-7327
www.pearlpaint.com
• Suppliers of art and craft materials. Purchase online or see website for store locations.

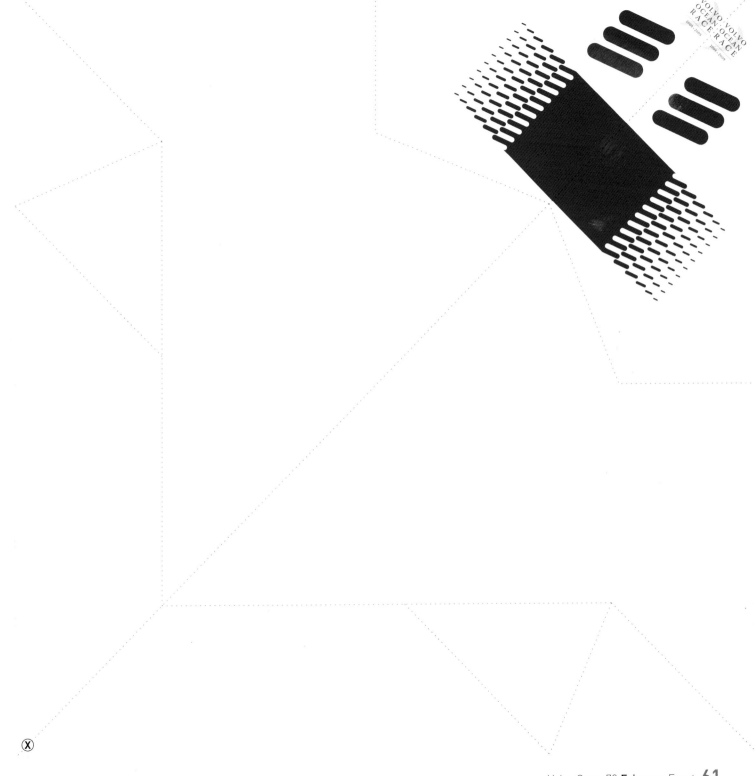

(X)

ERICSSON **〓**

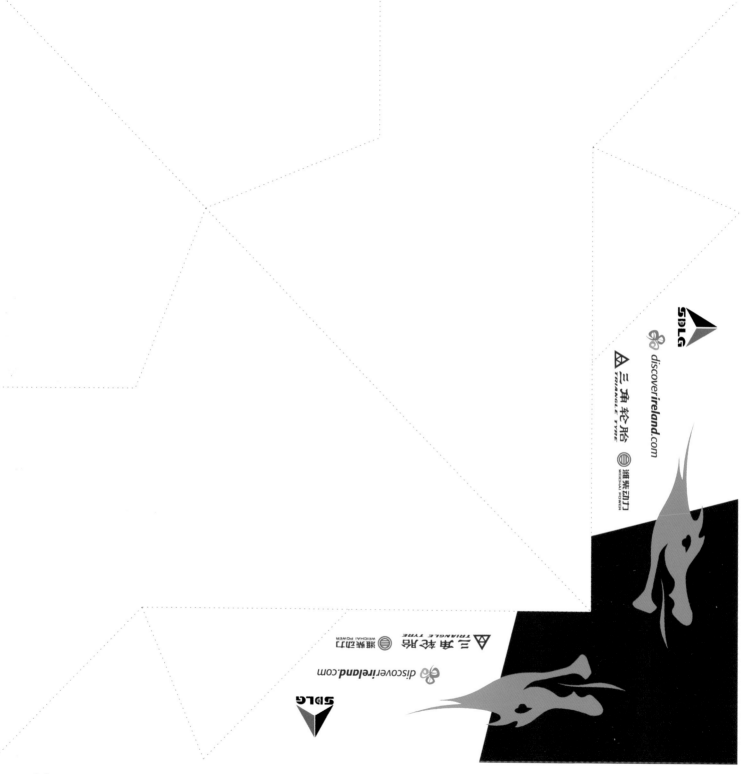

alinghi

alınghı

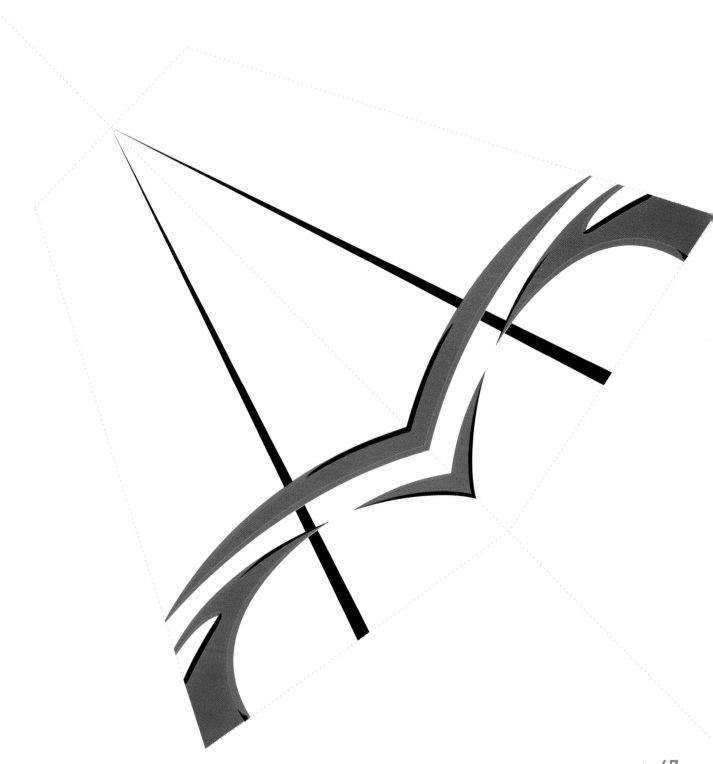

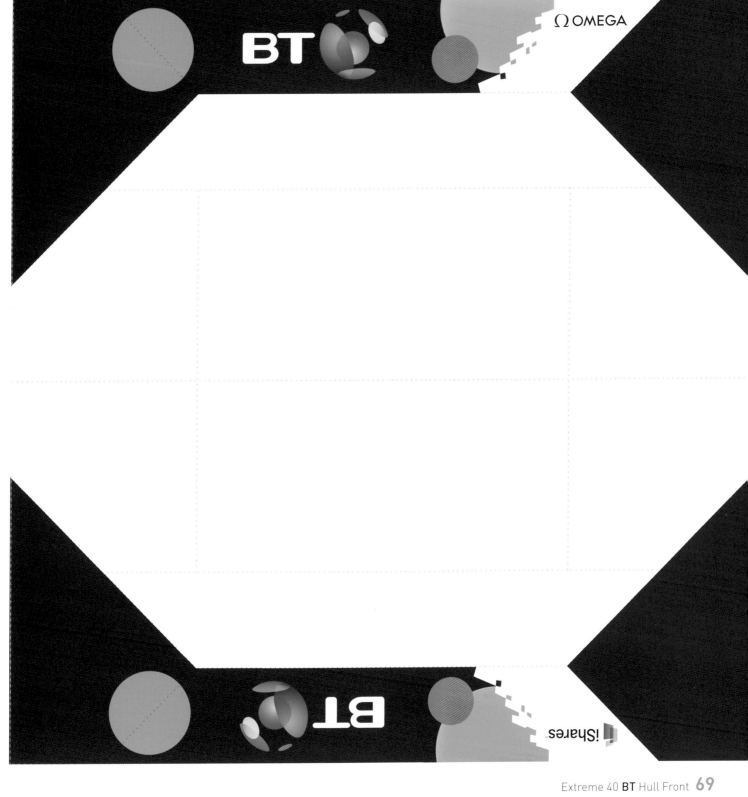

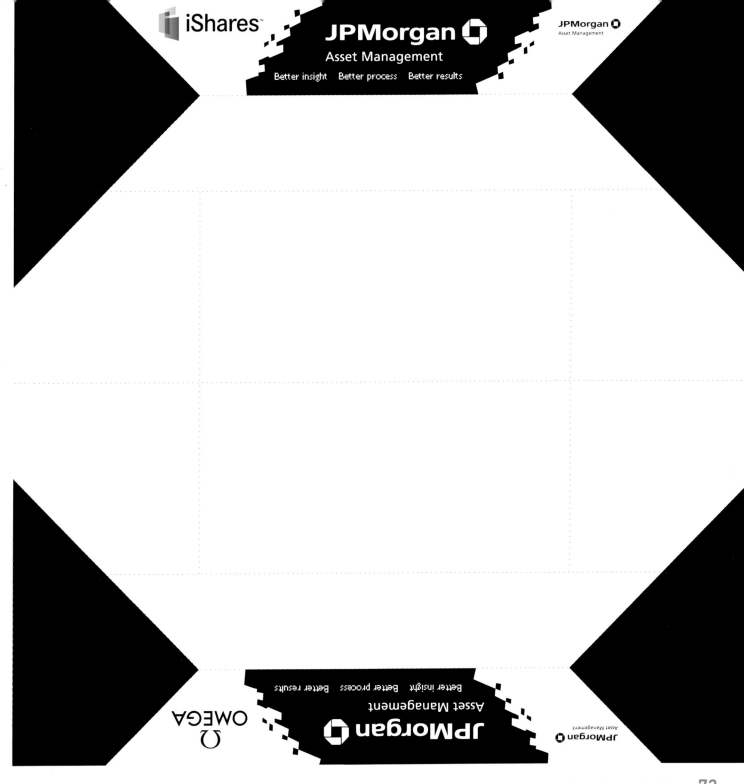

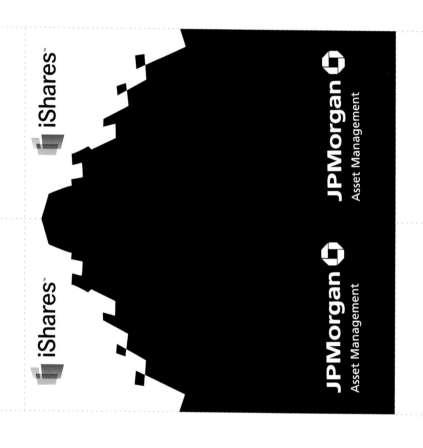

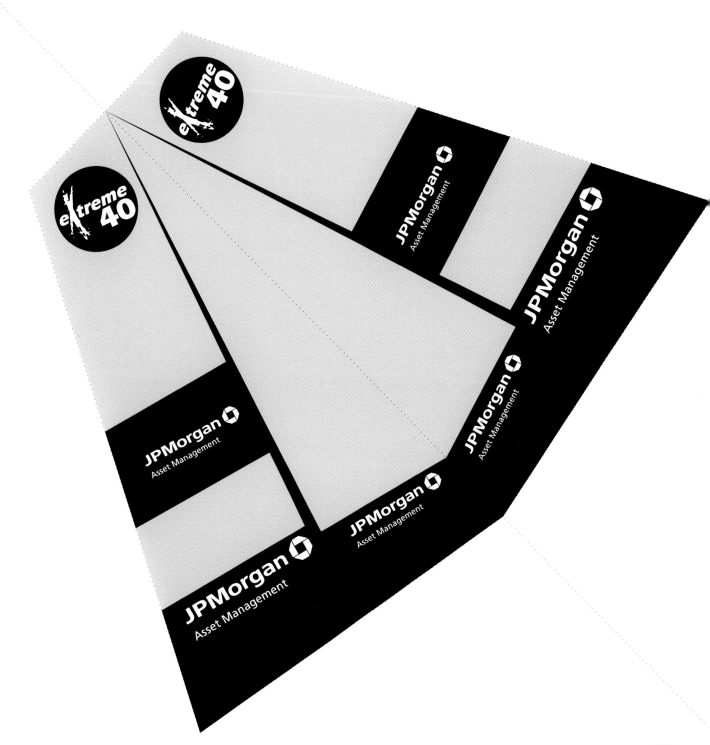

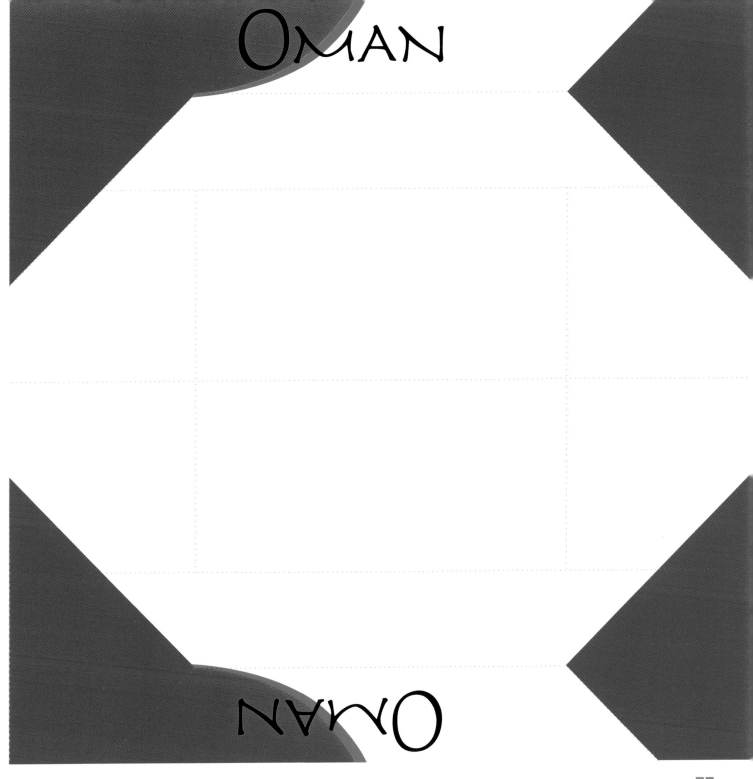

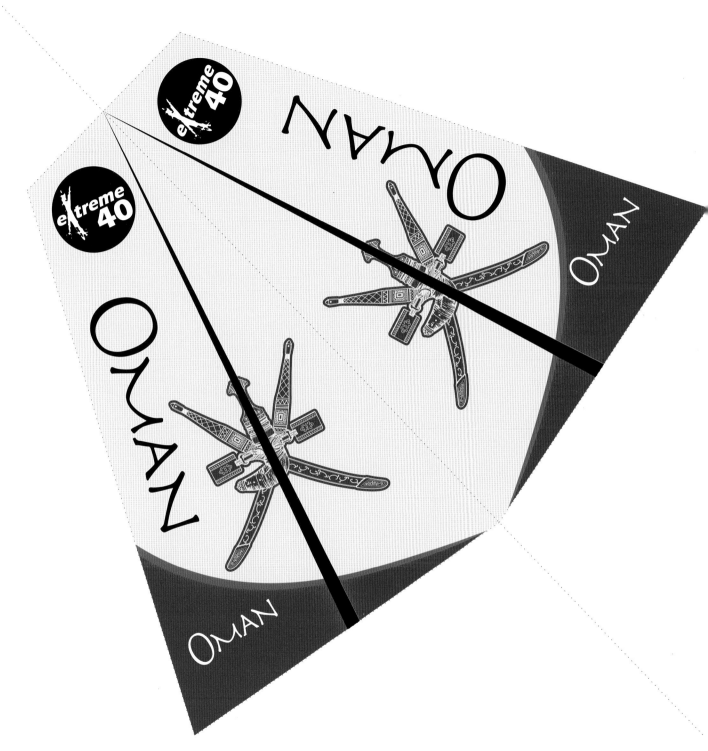

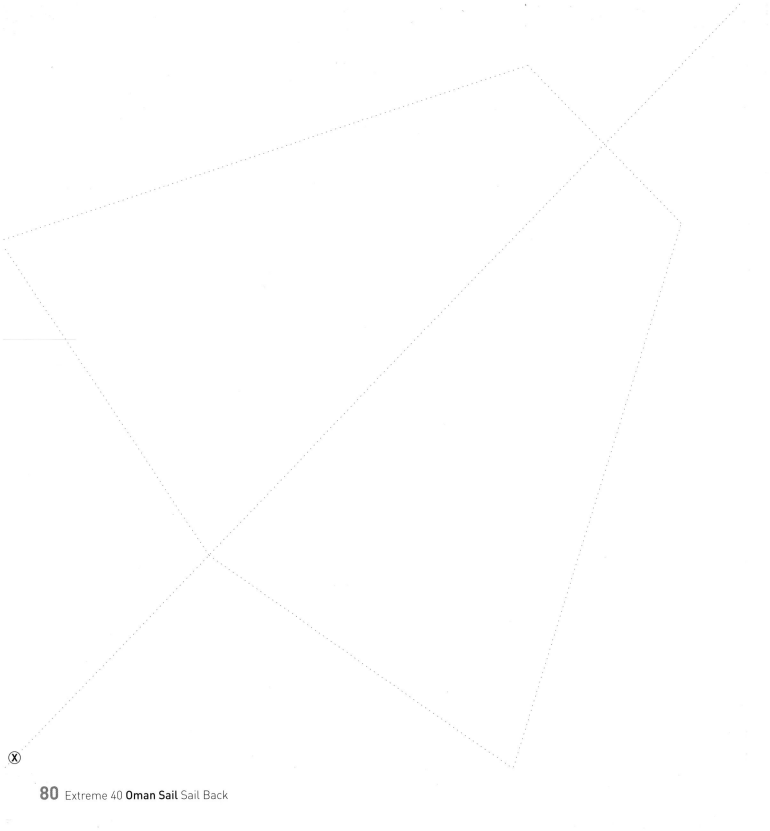